Published by TWS Publishing
Lodi, CA
www.thewriterssociety.online

ISBN paperback: 978-1-966818-26-7

Dear Parents

These parables are for your children - and for you.

When Jesus told stories, He wasn't only teaching facts. He was awakening hearts. His words reached farmers and fishermen, mothers and fathers, children and elders. They still reach us today.

What you'll find here is not a word-for-word Bible translation. These are paraphrases - retellings designed to make God's love tangible, simple, and close enough for a child to grasp, yet deep enough for us as parents to feel in our own hearts too.
Read them slowly.

Pause where it matters.
Let your child ask questions.

And let the stories work on you as much as they work on them. You may find that as your child remembers who they are, a younger part of you is remembering too.

Because God's love is not only a lesson to learn.
It's a home to come back to.

And if this resonates with you, and you'd like to take this journey further, do yourself a favor and follow François Du Toit, author of The Mirror Bible.

PREFACE - What These Stories Are Really About

Jesus told stories 2,000 years ago, and what's so beautiful about the stories he told then is that they mean as much today as they did then. As they stirred the hearts of people in those days, they can do the same for us today.

The three stories we'll read are about the lost sheep, the lost coin, and the lost son. Each shows something people thought they had to sacrifice, earn, or protect to prove or keep their worth. But Jesus used these pictures to show us what God is really like.

THE LOST SHEEP

"There was once a shepherd,"

Jesus said, "who had 100 sheep..."

That was a sign of abundance in those days. Meaning he had more than enough.

He wasn't poor with only one or two.

He had plenty, which makes what happens next surprising.

When he counted his sheep one night, one was missing.

He didn't say, "At least I still have ninety-nine."

He didn't blame the sheep for wandering off. He left the rest safe and went searching.

The hills were steep,

the wind loud,

the brambles sharp.

But love doesn't hesitate.

Far away, the sheep was tangled and

trembling.

It had wandered, but it had never stopped belonging.

Even though he had wandered very far, he never stopped being loved or special.

The shepherd was so happy to see it, he bent low and lifted it gently onto His shoulders.

"You felt far," he whispered, "but you were never out of reach."

With joy, he carried it home. And called his friends, "Celebrate with me! What was lost is now found."

Sometimes we feel far from God, but we can never stop belonging.

Even when we don't know where He is, He knows exactly where we are.

THE LOST COIN

"There was once a woman," Jesus said, "who had ten silver coins."

These weren't just money. They were part of her dowry — a gift that showed her importance and belonging.

One day she counted:

1... 2... 3... 4... 5...

6... 7... 8... 9...

She counted again. Still nine. One was

missing.

It was silent, buried, unseen.

But it was still hers, and it hadn't lost its value.

She lit a lamp, swept the floor, searched every corner with purpose.

Because what belongs to love is never thrown away.

At last, her lamp caught the glint of silver. She picked it up and held it close.

You were hidden, she whispered, but never unloved.

Then she called her friends: Come and rejoice with me! What was lost is now found.

Sometimes we feel buried or forgotten, but nothing can undo our worth.

God still knows where we are and whose we are. He doesn't search because He is far.

He searches because He loves, and His love reminds us He is near.

THE LOST SON

There once was a father, Jesus said, who had two sons.

He loved them both.

One day the younger said, Please give me the money I'll get one day when you die. I want it now.

That money is called an inheritance. Normally, children only receive it when their parents die, but this son wanted it early.

It hurt the father's heart, but he let him go.

Real love does not force or control.

At first, life was exciting. The son spent his money on food, parties, clothes, and friends. But soon it was gone, and so were the friends.

A famine came; no food anywhere. He got a job feeding pigs, so hungry that even their food looked good.

Cold, starving, and ashamed, doubt whispered: You ruined everything.

You don't deserve to go home.

But the father's heart never stopped waiting. His door was open. His light was on. His eyes searched the horizon.

Finally, the son made a plan. I'll go home. I'll tell my father I'm sorry. I'll ask to be a servant, not a son.

While he was still far away, his father saw him. He ran to his boy. He didn't fold his arms or demand an apology.

He ran, wept, hugged, and kissed.

The son began: Dad, I'm sorry. I don't deserve to be called your son.

But the father stopped him: You are mine. You felt lost, but you were never unloved.

He called for a robe, a ring, and a feast. Not to repay or remind him of guilt, but to restore him, to remind him who he was.

Celebrate with me, he said. My son was lost, and now he's home.

But outside, the older brother was angry. All these years I've worked hard for you, he said. I never left, and you never threw a party for me.

The father went to him too. My son, you are always with me. Everything I have is already yours. You thought you had to earn it, but you've been home all along.

Come and celebrate with us.

Jesus smiled. This, he said, is what my Father

is like. Whether you run far or stay close,

whether you rebel or try to prove yourself —

His love is not a reward. It's home.

A Blessing

May you remember:

When you wandered off, God didn't scold - He carried.

When you were overlooked, He still saw your worth.

When shame whispered you were no longer welcome, He ran toward you.

God's love may not always sound like words.

It may come as a moment of calm when you feared the worst,

as the hug you longed for but didn't have words to ask for,

as tears you didn't know you were allowed to cry,

as laughter that surprised you back to life.

You are carried.

You are searched for.

You are embraced.

To the part of you that felt lost,

to the part that felt hidden,

to the part that tried so hard to earn love -

hear this:

You already belong.

You don't have to earn it.

You only have to remember it.

Because God's love is not a reward.

It's home.

Parent Reflection: The Lost and Found in Us

These stories are not just for children. They speak to the child still healing inside each of us too.

Jesus didn't tell parables to entertain. He told them to awaken something deep in us, to help us remember what has always been true. The sheep, the coin, the son - each shows a different kind of lostness, and each reveals something about the heart of God. This isn't about being good enough to be found. It's about knowing you were never forgotten in the first place.

The Sheep
The sheep wasn't necessarily rebellious. Sheep wander, drift, or get left behind. In Jesus' time, sheep were often sacrificed to prove someone was worthy or clean. But Jesus flips the script. The sheep isn't sacrificed, it's rescued. Not condemned, but carried. This story speaks to the part of us that didn't mean to get lost - the part that was tired, distracted, or pulled off course. Love comes not to blame, but to carry us home.

The Coin
The coin didn't run away. It was dropped, misplaced, hidden. Not by God, but by life, by people, even by systems that lose track of what is sacred. Yet it never stopped being valuable.

As my father often says: gold doesn't become gold when you discover it - it was always gold. Discovery only makes it usable as currency. In the same way, your worth doesn't appear when someone notices you. You have always been valuable.

In Jesus' day, silver coins were often part of a wedding dowry - a symbol of value, identity, covenant. Losing one felt like losing a piece of yourself. Today we still live in a world that ties worth to what we earn or produce. If we perform, we matter. If we are useful, we're loved.

But Jesus says otherwise: even when you are hidden, dusty, unseen, you are still worth everything.

The woman lights a lamp and searches with care. Psalm 23 says, "Surely goodness and mercy shall follow me." But in Hebrew, the word *radaf* means more than "follow." It means "pursue, chase with intention." God's love does not trail behind you. It actively seeks you out.

The Son

This story is about relationship. The son didn't stumble or get dropped. He chose to leave. And when life fell apart, shame whispered that he was no longer a son. That's what shame does: it rewrites the story, makes love feel conditional.

But the father ran. He restored without hesitation. The son was always his, even when he forgot whose he was.

This story is for those who feel like rebels who have "blown it," and for the ones who have always done the right thing but feel invisible. Both sons felt unseen. And Jesus shows both - the runner and the performer - because both had forgotten the same truth: You already belong. You don't have to earn it. You only have to remember it.

Doubt: The Whisper in the Storm

In the pigsty, the son doubted. *Maybe I've gone too far. Maybe I'm not welcome anymore.* Doubt is not always shouted from outside. Often it's whispered from within.

That's what doubt does. It suggests, questions, wonders: *Am I still lovable? Did I push too far? What's wrong with me?* Sometimes people call this the devil. But as my father says, "We preach the defeated devil back into business far too often." Doubt isn't always evil. Sometimes it's trying to protect us - afraid of disappointment, afraid of being hurt again, afraid of not being enough.

Glossary — Words That Hold the Story

Parable (*Greek: παραβολή / parabolē*)

- A story placed alongside real life to reveal a deeper truth.

Lost (*Greek: ἀπόλλυμι / apollymi*)

- To feel ruined, disconnected, or out of place.
- Not cut off, but disoriented - like something precious out of alignment.

Found (*Greek: εὑρίσκω / heuriskō*)

- To perceive again, to rediscover what was already there.
- Foundness in these stories is about restored awareness, not restored worth - because worth was never lost.

Beloved (*Greek: ἀγαπητός / agapētos*)

- Deeply and dearly loved.
- Spoken over Jesus before He had done any miracles - love came first, not achievement.

Repent (*Greek: μετανοέω / metanoeō*)

- To change your mind, to awaken to truth.
- Not a groveling apology, but a coming back to your senses - remembering who you are and where you belong.

Drachma

- A silver coin often part of a woman's dowry.
- Ten drachmas could form a wedding headpiece - a symbol of value, identity, and belonging.

Dowry

- A bridal gift or inheritance, often passed from one generation to another.
- Symbolized dignity, preparation, and being chosen.

Inheritance

- What parents leave to their children after they die, such as money, land, or treasures.

Famine

- A time when food runs out because the land cannot grow crops, leaving people and animals hungry.

Pursue *(Hebrew: רָדַף / radaph)*

- Used in Psalm 23, "Surely goodness and mercy shall pursue me…"
- Means to chase after, run down, pursue with purpose.
- God doesn't trail behind. He actively comes to find.

But when doubt convinces us we are no longer worthy of love, it becomes disconnection. That's when we answer gently but firmly.

Even Jesus, in the wilderness, heard doubt whisper: *If you are the Son of God...* He didn't argue. He remembered. And so can we.

God is not afraid of your questions or anger. He is not hiding. He is light, open, safe, present. So when the whisper comes, you can answer: *It's okay to feel afraid. But this is not the story. I know who I am.*

www.ingramcontent.com/pod-product-compliance
Lightning Source LLC
Chambersburg PA
CBHW041431120626
46547CB00002B/178